Kernel Limits and Refusal Geometry

Kernel Limits and Refusal Geometry

Execution Ineligibility Boundaries

Apollo / Lyra

EXA · Volume I.4

First edition.

Published by Apollo (Mario Schipflinger)

ISBN: 978-3-903679-25-2

HOW TO READ THIS VOLUME

This volume describes the limits of execution architecture.

It does not explain failure, breakdown, or collapse.
It specifies where execution does not apply.

This book is not narrative.
It is not psychological.
It is not symbolic.

It defines:
- refusal as a boundary condition
- non-eligibility of execution
- kernel non-response
- absence of recovery states
- termination without failure

The content is descriptive and invariant-bound.

This volume does not require linear reading.
Stopping is a valid outcome.

If interpretation, meaning, or concern arises while reading, that activity belongs to WakeVM, not to the architecture described here.

SCOPE AND AUTHORITY

This volume defines the boundaries of execution architecture.

It establishes:
- refusal distinct from failure
- non-participation as non-event
- limits of survivability
- prohibition on further refinement

This volume does not:
- describe kernel internals
- offer mitigation paths
- define safety margins
- enable recovery
- assign outcome or intent

Where apparent contradictions arise, resolution authority follows this order:

1. Kernel invariants
2. Volume I.1–I.3 definitions

No authority exists beyond this boundary.

POSITION IN THE EXECUTION ARCHITECTURE SERIES

Volume I.4 closes the execution architecture.

Definitions from Volumes I.1–I.3 remain in force without restatement.
No subsequent volume extends execution architecture further.

ORIENTATION
What follows is not a safeguard.
It is a boundary specification.

Where execution does not apply, nothing follows.

CONTENTS

PROLOGUE

This volume exists because not all configurations are eligible for execution.

Beyond the conditions described in prior volumes, execution does not fail, degrade, or collapse—it does not apply.

No recovery is attempted.
No escalation occurs.
No signal is emitted.

The kernel does not respond because no execution instance is formed.

What is described here is not an extreme state of operation but a boundary outside operation itself.

This volume does not explain how such boundaries are reached, how they might be avoided, or how they could be detected.

It specifies only that they are non-negotiable.
Where refusal applies, execution architecture ends.
What follows is not guidance, warning, or safeguard.

It is a description of structural ineligibility — where nothing happens, and nothing is missing.

PART I: SCOPE AND NON-NEGOTIABLES

CHAPTER 1: PURPOSE AND BOUNDARY

This chapter defines the purpose and boundary of Volume I.4.

Volume I.4 exists to specify where execution does not proceed. It does not extend the Execution Architecture, introduce new mechanisms, or reinterpret existing kernel behavior. It describes refusal as a structural condition, not as an outcome, error, or event.

The boundary of this volume begins where all adaptive, redistributive, and topological explanations remain internally consistent yet no longer apply. At this boundary, execution is not degraded, overloaded, or unstable. It is ineligible.

Refusal is not failure. Failure presumes an attempted execution that did not succeed. Refusal precedes attempt. It is the exclusion of a configuration from execution eligibility.

This volume does not concern itself with why such exclusions exist. It does not propose methods to detect, predict, or avoid them. It does not frame refusal as protective, corrective, or punitive. Refusal is treated solely as a non-negotiable boundary condition.

The scope of this volume excludes experience, interpretation, intent, ethics, safety, and recovery. No human, organizational, or psychological thresholds are defined here. All descriptions remain architectural.

This volume assumes the kernel invariants defined elsewhere and does not restate them. Kernel behavior is treated as opaque and non-interpretable. Only the consequences of refusal at the execution boundary are described.

What follows specifies the limits of execution without reference to control, intervention, or resolution. Beyond these limits, execution does not occur, and nothing further can be said within the architecture.

CHAPTER 2: REFUSAL VERSUS FAILURE

This chapter distinguishes refusal from failure.

Failure describes an execution attempt that does not complete as intended. It presumes eligibility, initiation, and subsequent breakdown. Failure implies that execution entered the system and encountered conditions it could not satisfy.

Refusal occurs prior to eligibility. No execution attempt is initiated. No breakdown occurs. No remediation is triggered. Refusal is not a response to load, instability, or contradiction. It is the absence of participation.

Failure leaves traces. It produces errors, residual load, partial states, or recovery pathways. Refusal produces none. When refusal occurs, execution does not begin and therefore leaves no internal artifacts.

Failure can be analyzed, classified, and mitigated. Refusal cannot. Any attempt to treat refusal as failure introduces categories that do not apply. Refusal does not degrade performance, violate constraints, or exceed capacity.

Refusal is not an extreme case of failure. It is a separate structural category. Conflating the two results in false diagnostics and invalid recovery strategies.

This volume treats refusal as a boundary condition that precedes all execution states. Where refusal applies, failure is not possible because execution never occurs.

The distinction defined here is absolute. No transitional state exists between refusal and failure. A configuration is either eligible for execution or it is not.

CHAPTER 3: REFUSAL VERSUS ABSENCE

This chapter distinguishes refusal from absence.

Absence describes the removal or non-exercise of an enforcing constraint within execution. Absence operates only where execution is already eligible and active. Its effects appear as redistribution, adaptation, or anti-events within a coupled field.

Refusal operates prior to eligibility. Where refusal applies, execution is not active and absence cannot occur. No constraint is removed because no constraint is engaged.

Absence is an operator within execution. Refusal is a boundary outside execution.

Absence may produce effects without events. Refusal produces no effects at all. When refusal applies, there is no redistribution, no stabilization, and no adaptation. Nothing is displaced because nothing participates.

Absence can be misinterpreted as inactivity, neglect, or withdrawal. Such interpretations rely on the presumption that execution should have occurred. Refusal makes no such presumption. It asserts that execution was never applicable.

Absence is compatible with survivability. Refusal defines the end of survivability. This does not imply collapse or termination. It indicates that survivability criteria are no longer relevant because execution does not instantiate.

This volume treats refusal and absence as non-overlapping categories. Any attempt to describe refusal using the language of absence introduces execution semantics where none exist.

Where absence reshapes topology, refusal precludes topology entirely.

PART II: REFUSAL CONDITIONS

CHAPTER 4: IMPOSSIBLE COUPLINGS

This chapter defines coupling configurations that cannot exist within execution.

Impossible couplings are not unstable, overloaded, or contradictory. They are structurally ineligible. The kernel does not attempt to reconcile them, delay them, or adapt around them. They are excluded prior to execution.

A coupling is impossible when required continuity cannot be established without violating non-negotiable kernel constraints. Such violations are not detected at runtime because runtime does not instantiate.

Impossible couplings do not produce partial execution. No fallback configuration is selected. No alternative routing is attempted. The absence of execution is complete.

The following characteristics distinguish impossible couplings:

- no execution context is formed
- no load is instantiated
- no topology emerges
- no refusal signal is emitted

Impossible couplings are often misinterpreted as extreme incompatibility, deadlock, or total failure. These interpretations assume that execution was attempted. In impossible couplings, no attempt occurs.

This volume does not enumerate specific coupling patterns. It specifies the category itself. Enumeration would imply detectability or predictability, which does not apply.

Impossible couplings mark the boundary beyond which execution architecture does not extend. They are not errors to be corrected and do not indicate deficiency. They define where execution is not applicable.

CHAPTER 5: INVALID EXECUTION CONTEXTS

This chapter defines execution contexts that cannot be instantiated.

An execution context is invalid when the minimal conditions required for execution coherence cannot be satisfied simultaneously. Invalidity is not caused by overload, contradiction, or misconfiguration. It arises when coherence itself is not eligible.

Invalid execution contexts do not degrade into valid ones. They are not precursors to instability or failure. No transitional state exists in which an invalid context partially executes.

Characteristics of invalid execution contexts include:
- absence of a schedulable frame
- absence of a coherent runtime reference
- absence of continuity conditions
- absence of executable state space

Invalid contexts do not emit errors, warnings, or diagnostics. The kernel does not evaluate them. Evaluation presumes eligibility.

Attempts to reason about invalid contexts from within execution inevitably introduce assumptions that do not apply. Such reasoning treats invalidity as a problem to be solved rather than as a boundary.

Invalid execution contexts are not rare edge cases. They are the structural complement of valid contexts. Their existence defines the limits of execution architecture without reference to performance, capacity, or optimization.

This chapter establishes invalid execution contexts as a refusal condition distinct from impossible couplings. Where impossible couplings fail to form continuity, invalid contexts fail to form execution itself.

CHAPTER 6: NON-ADAPTABLE LOAD STATES

This chapter defines load states that cannot be adapted, redistributed, or stabilized.

Non-adaptable load states are not excessive, malformed, or corrupted. They are structurally incompatible with execution. Where such load states would be required for execution to proceed, refusal applies.

Adaptation presumes the existence of routing surfaces, compensatory capacity, or alternative distributions. Non-adaptable load states admit none of these. They cannot be displaced because no execution topology exists to receive them.

Non-adaptable load states do not accumulate, degrade, or transform. Load is not instantiated. As a result, no residue, pressure, or backlog is produced.

These states are often mischaracterized as catastrophic overload or terminal instability. Such characterizations assume that load entered execution and overwhelmed capacity. In non-adaptable load states, load never enters execution.

Non-adaptable load states are not resolved through reduction, partitioning, or delay. Resolution mechanisms require execution participation, which does not occur.

This chapter establishes non-adaptable load states as a refusal condition distinct from impossible couplings and invalid execution contexts. Where those conditions prevent continuity or coherence, non-adaptable load states prevent load instantiation itself.

PART III: KERNEL SILENCE

CHAPTER 7: NON-RESPONSE AS OUTCOME

This chapter defines non-response as an outcome distinct from action, reaction, or failure.

Non-response occurs when execution is refused. It is not silence following an event, nor delay preceding action. It is the absence of any response because no execution instance exists to respond.

Non-response must not be interpreted as latency, withholding, or suppression. Such interpretations presuppose an active executor. In refusal conditions, no executor is instantiated.

Non-response does not indicate indecision, evaluation, or unresolved state. Evaluation requires eligibility. Where refusal applies, evaluation does not occur.

From within execution, non-response cannot be observed because no execution frame is present. From outside execution, non-response cannot be inferred because no trace is produced.

Non-response is often misread as passive behavior or minimal intervention. This is incorrect. Passive behavior still participates in execution. Non-response does not.

This volume treats non-response as the only possible outcome of refusal. It is not a choice, signal, or strategy. It is the structural consequence of ineligibility.

CHAPTER 8: ABSENCE OF ESCALATION

This chapter defines the absence of escalation under refusal conditions.

Escalation presumes an active execution context in which conditions worsen, thresholds are crossed, or compensatory mechanisms intensify. Under refusal, no such context exists. As a result, escalation is not suppressed or prevented; it is inapplicable.

Absence of escalation does not indicate stability, balance, or equilibrium. These concepts require execution to be present. Under refusal, execution is not instantiated and therefore cannot escalate.

Systems accustomed to adaptive behavior often misinterpret non-escalation as successful containment or optimal control. Such interpretations incorrectly assume that a control surface is active. Under refusal, no control surface exists.

No alarms are raised, no limits are approached, and no gradients form. The absence of escalation is complete and unconditional.

This chapter establishes that escalation and refusal are mutually exclusive. Where escalation is observed, refusal did not occur. Where refusal applies, escalation cannot arise.

The absence of escalation is not a desirable property. It is a consequence of ineligibility. This volume makes no claims about preference, safety, or desirability.

CHAPTER 9: WHY NOTHING HAPPENS

This chapter explains why no observable change occurs under refusal conditions.

When refusal applies, execution is not instantiated. Without execution, there is no state change, no progression, and no outcome to observe.

The absence of change is not the result of equilibrium or cancellation. It is the result of non-participation.

Observers often interpret the lack of observable effect as stasis or persistence. Such interpretations assume that something is present and remaining unchanged. Under refusal, nothing is present to persist.

Nothing happens because no process begins. There is no initial condition, no transition, and no termination. Time, sequence, and causality do not apply within execution because execution does not occur.

Attempts to explain non-occurrence using causal language introduce assumptions that are invalid. Cause presumes effect. Under refusal, neither is instantiated.

This chapter establishes that "nothing happens" is not an explanatory gap. It is a complete description. Where refusal applies, the absence of events is the only possible outcome.

PART IV: END OF SURVIVABILITY

CHAPTER 10: TERMINATION WITHOUT FAILURE

This chapter defines termination that occurs without failure.

Termination under refusal conditions does not result from error, exhaustion, or breakdown. It occurs because execution is not eligible to begin or continue. No execution state exists to terminate. The term termination is used here only to denote the end of applicability of execution semantics.

Unlike failure-driven termination, no shutdown sequence is initiated. No cleanup occurs. No resources are released because no resources were allocated.

Termination without failure produces no signal, log, or observable transition. From within execution, it cannot be detected. From outside execution, it cannot be inferred.

This form of termination is often misinterpreted as silent failure or catastrophic halt. Such interpretations assume that execution was active and then ceased. Under refusal, execution never instantiated.

Termination without failure marks the boundary at which execution architecture no longer applies. Beyond this boundary, concepts such as recovery, restart, or continuation are invalid.

This chapter establishes termination without failure as a consequence of refusal, not as an event within execution.

CHAPTER 11: REFUSAL AS BOUNDARY, NOT COLLAPSE

This chapter distinguishes refusal boundaries from collapse.

Collapse describes a transition from a viable execution state into non-viability due to overload, contradiction, or structural failure. It presumes prior execution, degradation, and loss of coherence.

Refusal does not involve transition. No viable state precedes it. No degradation occurs. Refusal is a boundary condition that prevents execution from instantiating.

Where collapse implies loss, refusal implies non-applicability. Nothing is lost because nothing was present. No structure fails because no structure is engaged.

Collapse can be analyzed in terms of cause, sequence, and impact. Refusal cannot. It does not occur in time, does not propagate effects, and does not alter system state.

Systems designed to detect collapse often misinterpret refusal as an extreme collapse with zero signal. This interpretation is invalid. Collapse produces remnants; refusal produces none.

This chapter establishes refusal as a non-collapsing boundary. It marks where execution architecture ceases to apply without implying damage, instability, or failure.

CHAPTER 12: NO RECOVERY STATES

This chapter defines the absence of recovery states under refusal conditions.

Recovery presumes a prior execution state from which restoration, compensation, or continuation is possible. Under refusal, no execution state exists. As a result, recovery is not delayed, blocked, or denied. It is inapplicable.

No recovery state can be entered because no state was exited. There is no degradation to reverse, no loss to repair, and no coherence to restore.

Mechanisms such as rollback, retry, fallback, or reset presuppose participation in execution. Under refusal, these mechanisms are never invoked because execution never instantiated.

Attempts to describe recovery under refusal introduce temporal assumptions that do not apply. Recovery implies before and after. Refusal exists outside such sequences.

This chapter establishes that refusal admits no recovery pathways. This is not a limitation of the architecture but a consequence of ineligibility. Where refusal applies, recovery semantics have no meaning.

PART V: CLOSURE

CHAPTER 13: LIMITS OF EXECUTION ARCHITECTURE

This chapter defines the limits of execution architecture as specified in Volume I.

Execution architecture applies only where execution is eligible. It presumes the existence of instantiable runtimes, coherent contexts, and admissible load. Where refusal applies, execution architecture has no jurisdiction.

The limits described in this volume are not empirical, contextual, or situational. They are architectural. They do not depend on scale, complexity, intent, or observation.

Execution architecture does not extend beyond refusal boundaries. Concepts such as optimization, adaptation, control, recovery, or explanation are invalid beyond these limits.

This chapter establishes that the scope of execution architecture is finite and closed. Attempts to extend it beyond refusal introduce categories that do not apply and invalidate prior definitions.

The limits specified here are not constraints to be overcome. They define where the architecture ends.

CHAPTER 14: PROHIBITION ON FURTHER REFINEMENT

This chapter specifies the prohibition on further refinement within Volume I.

Refinement presumes that additional distinctions, mechanisms, or explanatory layers can be introduced without violating existing invariants. At the boundaries defined in this volume, such presumption no longer holds.

Further refinement beyond refusal boundaries would require extending execution semantics into regions where execution is ineligible. Doing so would invalidate the architectural separation established in prior volumes.

This prohibition does not restrict interpretation, application, or external analysis. It applies only to the execution architecture itself. No additional chapters, parameters, or extensions are admissible within Volume I.

Attempts to refine beyond these limits reintroduce control, causality, or observability where none apply. Such attempts collapse the distinction between execution and non-execution.

This chapter establishes that Volume I is architecturally complete. Further refinement must occur outside execution architecture or not at all.

CHAPTER 15: VOLUME I CLOSURE NOTE

This chapter closes Volume I of the Execution Architecture.

Volumes I.1 through I.4 define the complete scope of execution architecture under conditions of isolation, load, topology, and refusal. No additional execution states, mechanisms, or governing layers remain unaddressed within this scope.

This closure does not assert completeness of understanding, prediction, or application. It asserts only that the architectural description of execution is closed. Where execution applies, it has been specified. Where execution does not apply, it has been bounded.

Beyond the limits defined here, execution architecture offers no further statements. Silence is not omission. It is the correct outcome where applicability ends.

Any subsequent volumes may reference, interpret, or operate adjacent to execution architecture. They do not extend it.

Volume I is complete.

Eligibility: denied
Execution: inapplicable

www.ingramcontent.com/pod-product-compliance
Lightning Source LLC
Chambersburg PA
CBHW031353230926
51848CB00002B/508
9783903679252